Baby Moorhen makes a splash!

A story for children aged 1 – 8 years

Author: Hazel Douglas
Illustrator: Richard Johnson
Designer: Sally Geeve

For Ken and Paula
Hazel

For Leon, Zoe and Isla May
Richard

Published by Jill Rogers Associates, Cambridge, UK

First published April 2012

ISBN: 978-0-9560156-6-2

Baby Moorhen walked along the edge of the lake with his brothers and sisters. Sometimes he walked at the side of Mr and Mrs Moorhen. Sometimes he walked behind Mr and Mrs Moorhen. Suddenly he stopped.
He saw Mr and Mrs Tufted Duck and their ducklings on the lake. He started to count.

3

'One, two...
No, one, two, three, four...
No that's wrong, one, two, three...
Wait!
There were four a second ago.'

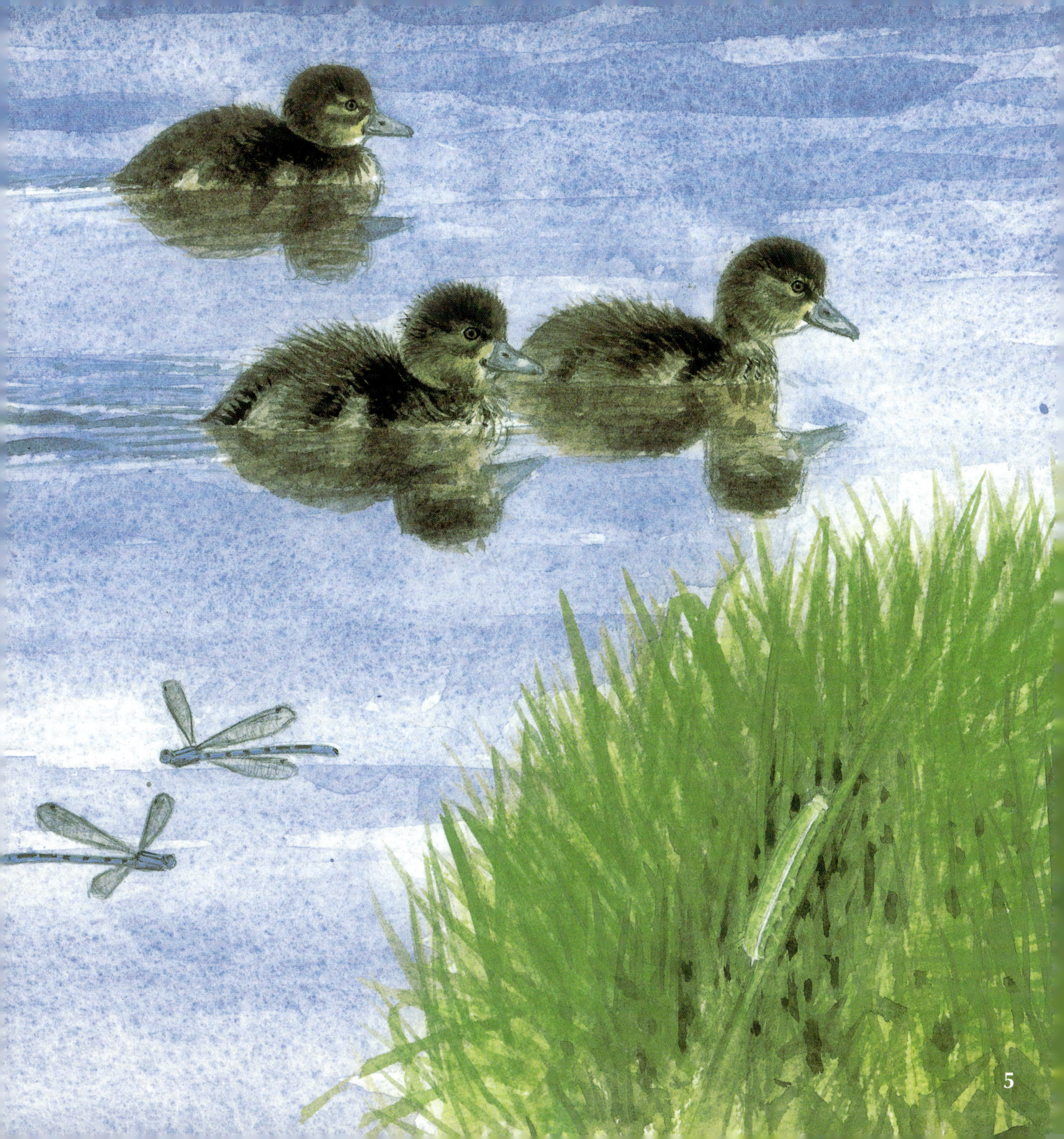

'One, two, three!
Where did they go?

Right, start again.
One...'

Then Baby Moorhen saw a different kind of family. It was Wendy with Roger and Dorothy, taking Rolly for a walk. John rushed up with a bag of duck food.

'Look! I bought this in the shop. I fed my birds in the garden this morning, so now I'm going to feed the ducks.' He threw some duck food near Mr and Mrs Moorhen.

9

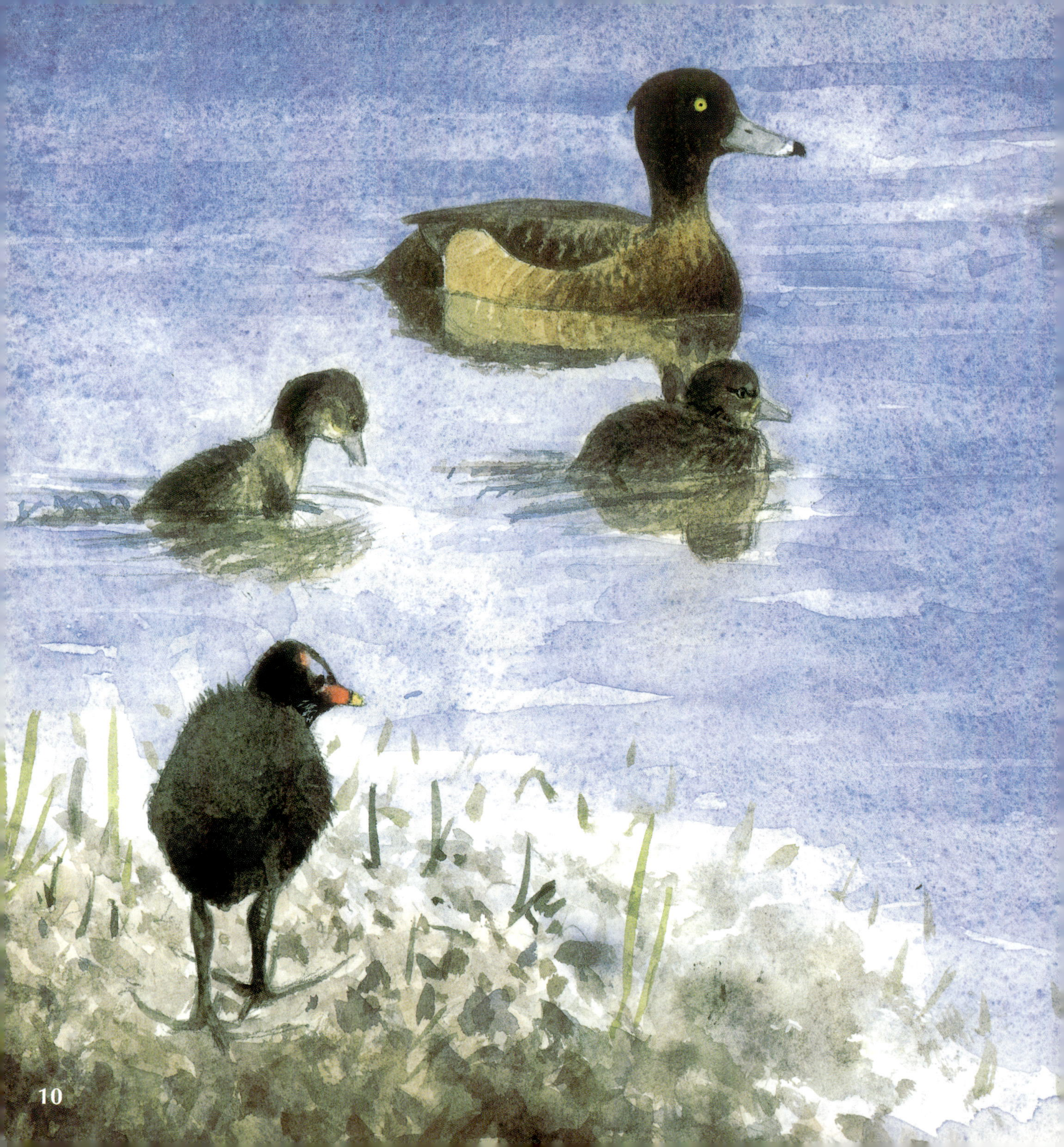

Wendy pointed to the middle of the lake.

'There's the Baby Tufted Ducks. They are already diving for their dinner like Mr and Mrs Tufted Duck.' Diving! So that was it! They kept disappearing because they went down underneath the water!

'Now you see them... now you don't' Baby Moorhen said to himself.

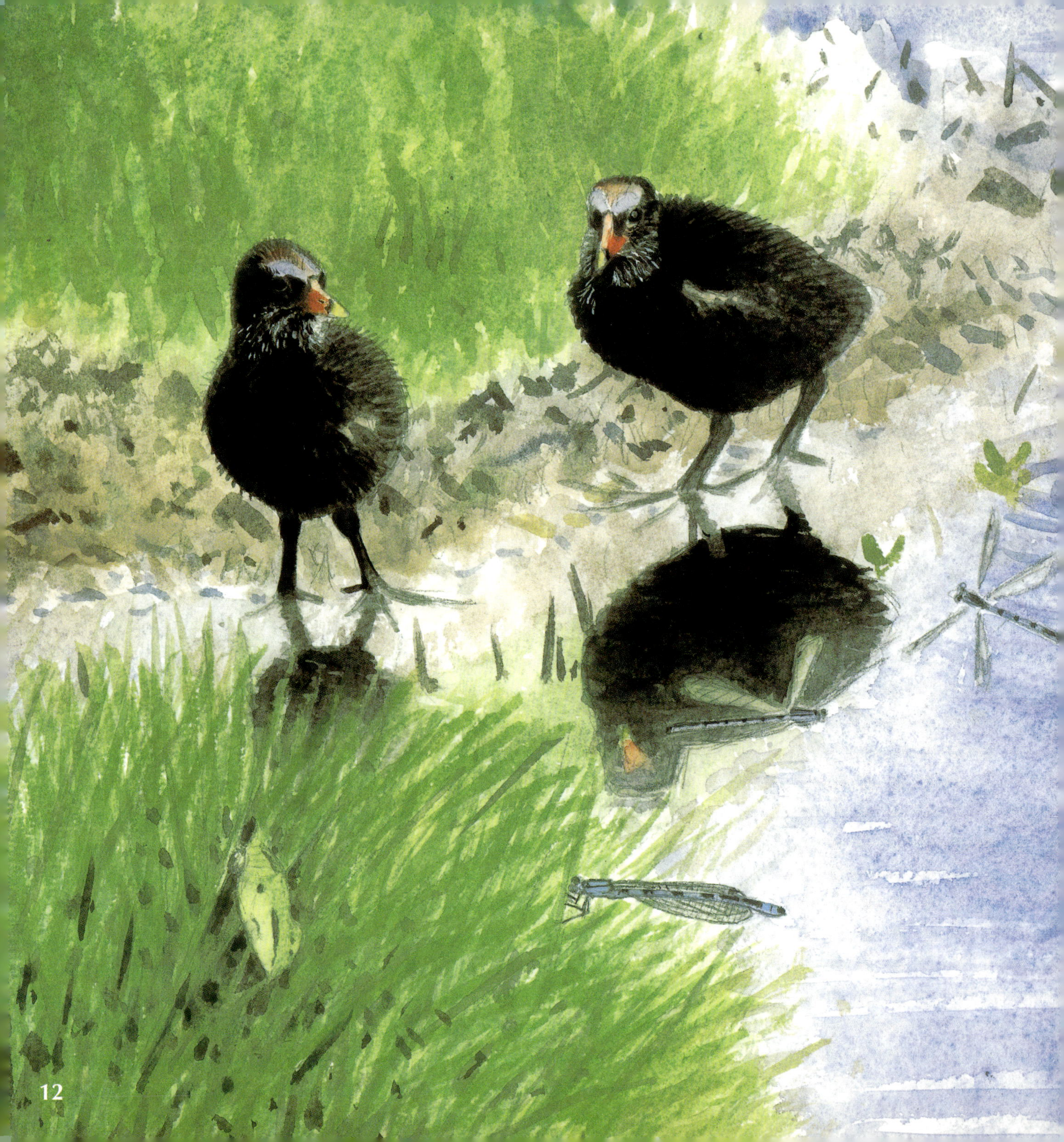

He turned and watched his brothers and sisters. One brother walked in the water, two sisters were swimming and his other brother walked on the bank.

'Hmmm' he thought to himself.
'I think I'll try being a Tufted Duck'.

He took a big breath, put his head under the water and tried to kick with his big feet.

Splash, splash, splash, splutter, splutter, splutter!

'Quick' Wendy shouted, 'That Baby Moorhen is drowning.'

Wendy and Roger ran to the water's edge with Rolly.

Mrs Moorhen looked round. She saw her Baby Moorhen splashing and splashing in the water with a big dog looking at him. She rushed over.

'Get away from my baby' she squawked. Baby Moorhen came up to breathe.

'I think he's ok now' said Roger.

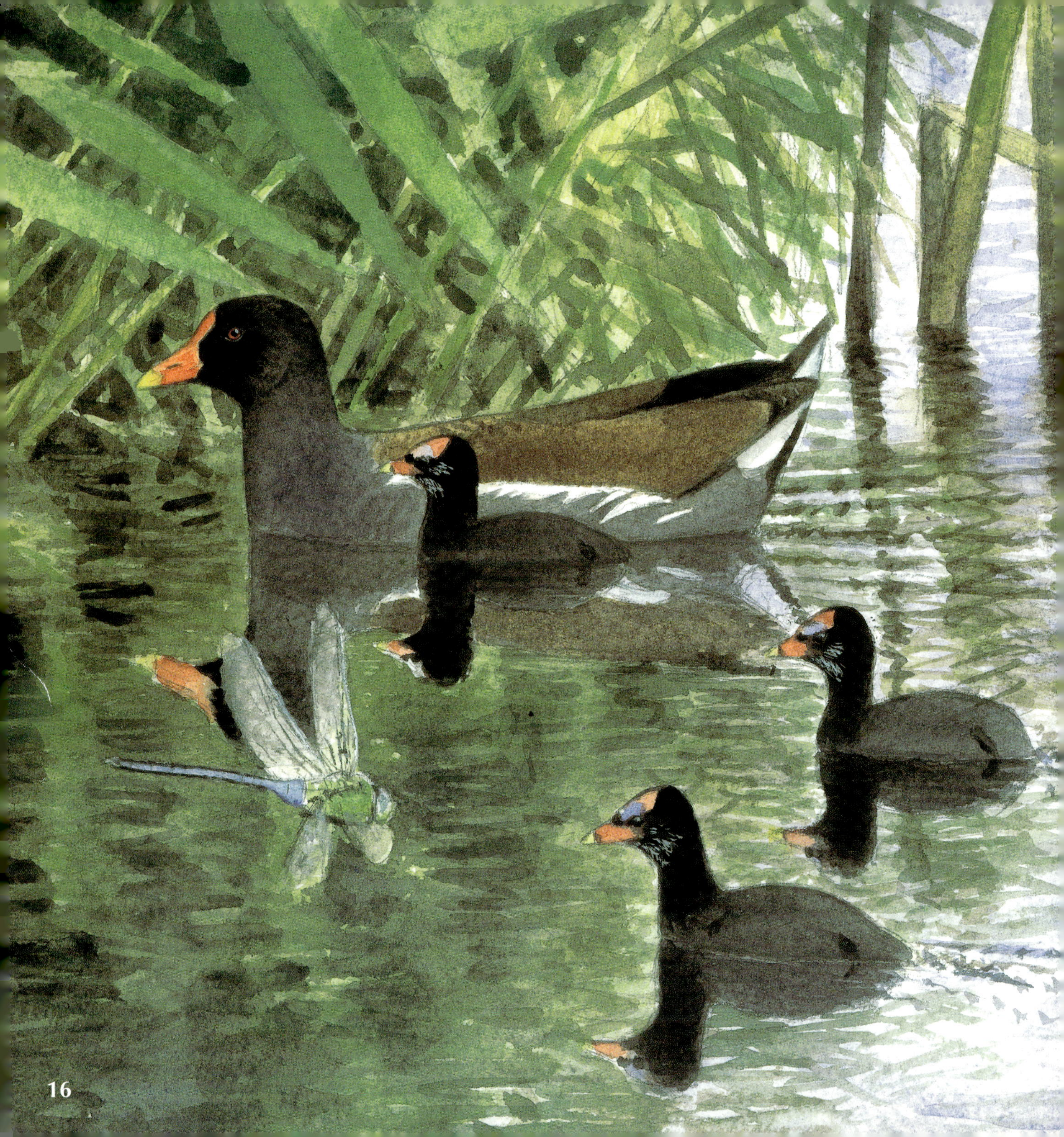

'Follow me,' said Mrs Moorhen 'You can't get away from the dog under the water.'

'What? I wasn't getting away from the dog. I was being a Tufted Duckling!'

'And how did that work out?' said Mrs Moorhen, exasperated.

'Terrible. I couldn't get under the water. I tried and tried and tried.'

'You don't have webbed feet! They dive because they eat stuff in the deep bit of the lake. We eat different stuff at the edge of the lake. Follow me and learn how to be a Moorhen first!'

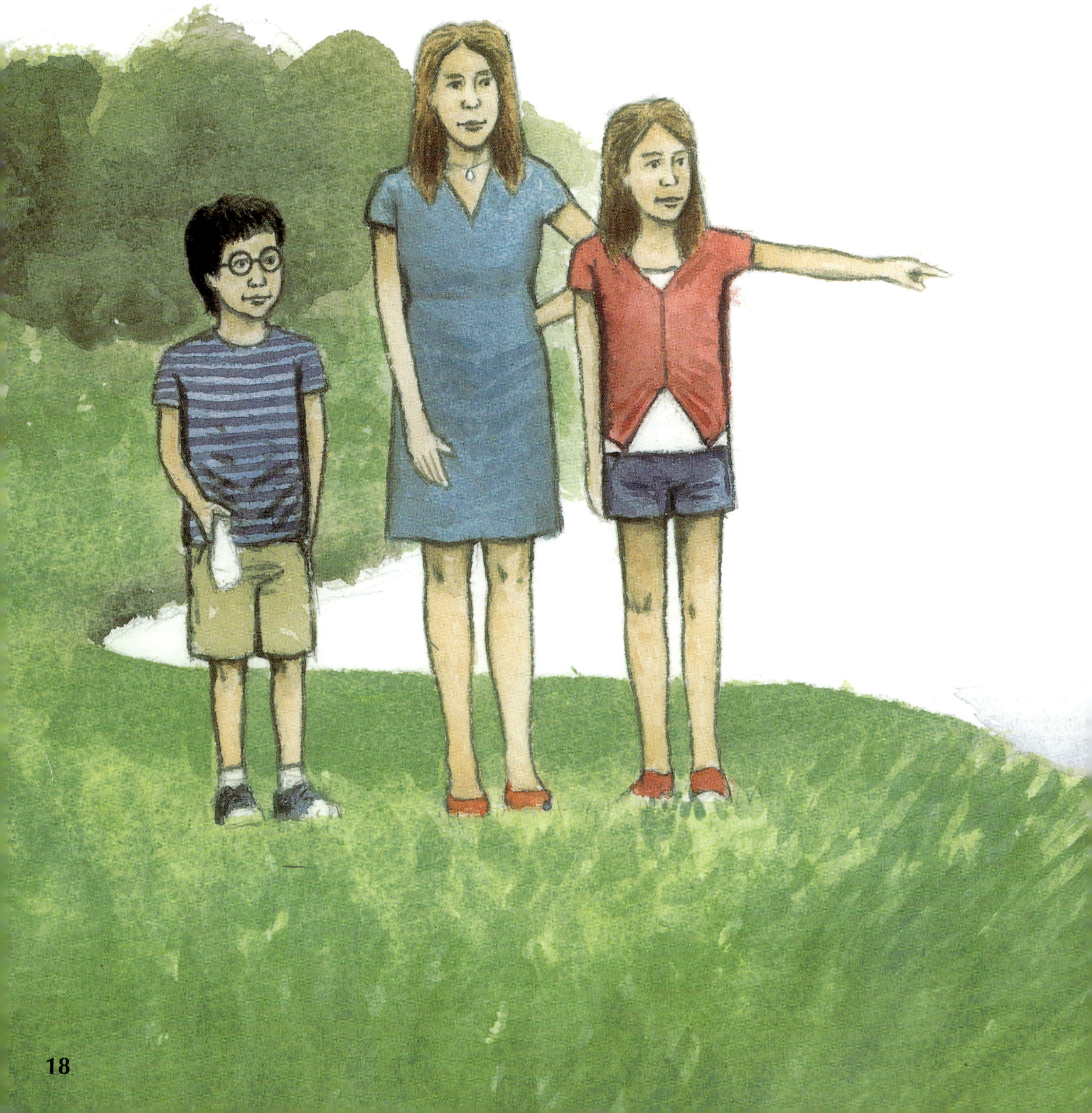

'That is one ugly duckling' said John.

'He's not a duckling. He's a Moorhen' said Dorothy.

'Look how handsome he will be one day' said Wendy.

'As lovely as a swan, but with lots more colours!' said Dorothy.

'Ugly duckling' whispered John.

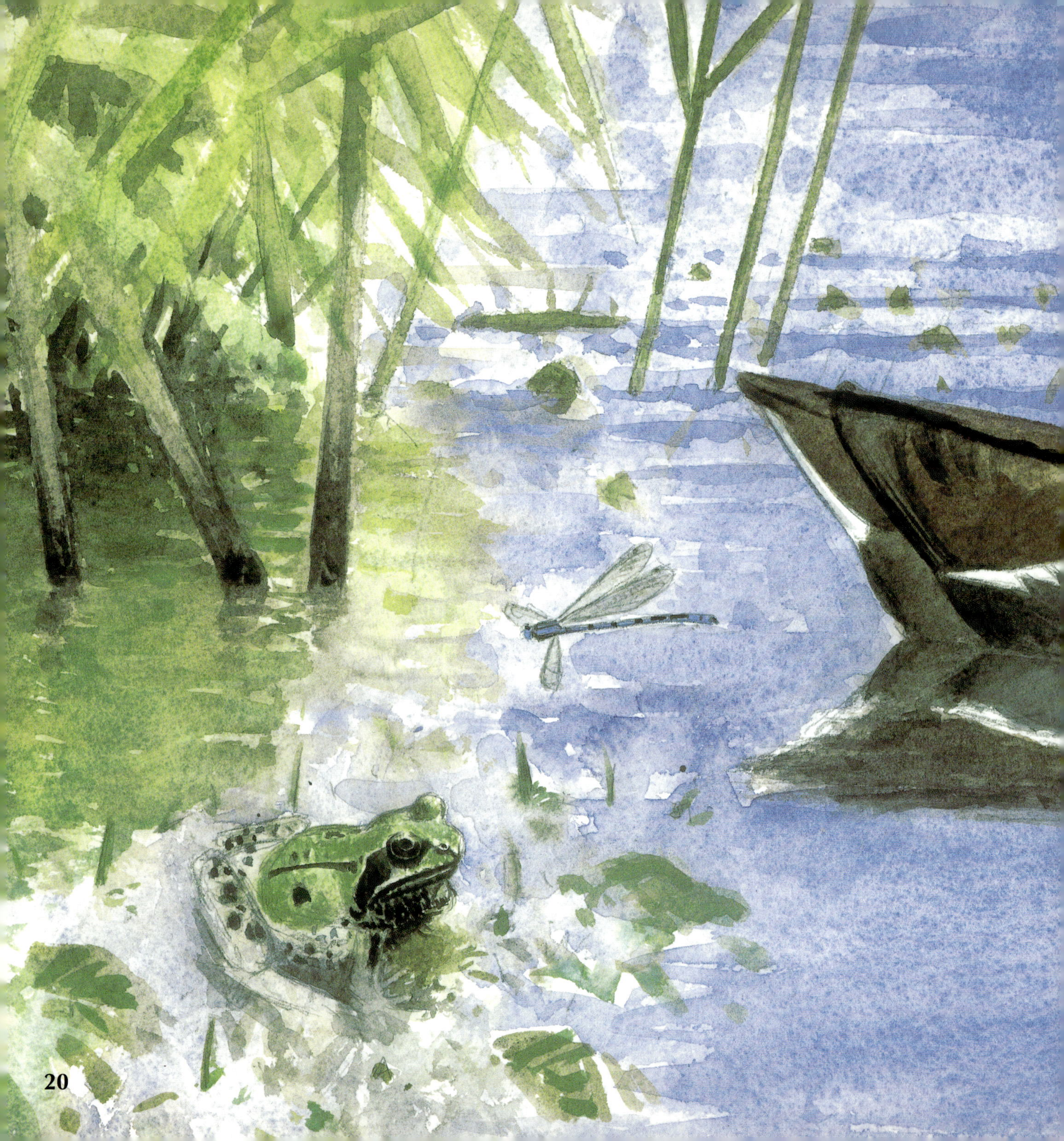

'Don't listen to him' said Mrs Moorhen.
'I love you just the way you are!'

More about Mr and Mrs Moorhen and Baby Moorhen

Mr Moorhen

Teenager Moorhen

Baby Moorhen

What do Mr and Mrs Moorhen and Baby Moorhen like to eat?

Mr and Mrs Moorhen eat lots of different things: insects, snails, berries, water plants, worms and more. Their big feet mean that they can often walk along the top of the water plants, finding snails and insects and eating the plants too. Baby Moorhen starts off with soft things like caterpillars and grubs.

Where do Mr and Mrs Moorhen and Baby Moorhen like to live?

Mr and Mrs Moorhen and Baby Moorhen live by the side of fresh water. You can see them by lakes, ponds, streams and in marshes… wherever there is wet land.

Who helps Mr and Mrs Moorhen bring up Baby Moorhen?

Mr and Mrs Moorhen often have 2 broods a year. When the babies in the second brood come along, the ones from the first brood are now teenagers. They do not look like Mr and Mrs Moorhen. Teenager Moorhen is brown. Teenager Moorhen helps his mum and dad with the new babies. This is very unusual in birds.

Teenager Moorhen doesn't know much about bringing up babies! He has to learn quickly. He will sometimes offer Baby Moorhen some hard food. Baby Moorhen will spit it out until Teenager Moorhen gives him some soft food, like grubs.

What differences can you see between Mr and Mrs Moorhen?

They look the same. They also look the same in summer and winter.

Can you see 5 differences between Mr Moorhen, Teenager Moorhen and Baby Moorhen?

1. Teenager Moorhen is brown. He has a white chin and throat.
2. Baby Moorhen is light blue on the top of his head.
3. Mr Moorhen has a dark brown back. Baby Moorhen is black all over.
4. Baby Moorhen is fluffy!
5. Mr Moorhen has more white on him than Baby Moorhen.

More about Mr and Mrs Tufted Duck and Baby Tufted Duck

Where do Mr and Mrs Tufted Duck and Baby Tufted Duck like to live?

They like to live on lakes and ponds, but you can also see them on estuaries and rivers. You don't often see them on streams because they like water to be at least 2 metres deep. They don't like water to be too deep though, so you won't find them on water deeper than about 15 metres.

What do Mr and Mrs Tufted Duck and Baby Tufted Duck like to eat?

They prefer animals. Not furry animals, but animals with shells like snails and freshwater mussels (molluscs) and insects. They will eat plants too. They dive to find their food, so they don't eat in the shallow water where Moorhens eat.

How long have Tufted Ducks been on Planet Earth?

Fossils have been found from about 500,000 years ago. Neanderthal Man was around from about 280,000 years ago, so he may have seen Tufted Ducks.

What do the Swedish call Tufted Ducks?

Vigg. This is the shortest name for a Tufted Duck. The longest name is in French... *Fuligule Morillon*.

Can you spot three differences between Mr Tufted Duck and Mrs Tufted Duck?

1. Mr Tufted Duck has a blue/black head.
2. Mrs Tufted Duck has a smaller tuft.
3. Mr Tufted Duck has white sides.

Mr Tufted Duck

Mrs Tufted Duck

Baby Tufted Duck

You can visit websites to find out more about birds.

Why not try: Royal Society for the Protection of Bird www.rspb.org.uk/wildlife/birdguide
British Trust for Ornithology www.bto.org
British Garden Birds www.garden-birds.co.uk/birds

Have you spotted the other creat

Find the Meadow Brown Butterfly (p21)

The Meadow Brown Butterfly is common. It lives on grassland, where there is grass and meadow flowers... not your lawn, unless you leave an unmown patch. This is because it needs a mix of taller grasses for its caterpillars and certain flowers with nectar for itself. Its favourite nectar is from knapweed, thistles and brambles, but it also likes buttercups and yarrow. Most butterflies won't fly in dull weather, but the Meadow Brown will even fly in drizzly rain.

Can you find the Meadow Brown Caterpillar? (p5)

The Meadow Brown Caterpillar eats different sorts of grasses. It turns green as it eats more grass! It stays as a caterpillar over the winter, living in clumps of grass.

Can you find the Meadow Brown Chrysalis? (p12)

The caterpillar turns into a chrysalis after it has moulted 5 times. The chrysalis turns into a butterfly after 3 to 4 weeks.

Common Blue Damselfly (p5)

The Common Blue Damselfly is easy to see because it lives on anything watery in the UK, including your pond if you have one. It is around between May and September. It eats insects and likes to rest on plants near water. It has a thick blue stripe on the bit below its head, on its thorax. It is about 3 cm long. The larvae are called nymphs and live in the water. They climb up a stem when they are ready to turn into a damselfly.